WHAT WOULD YOU BE

Published by:
Boolarong Press
655 Toohey Road
Salisbury Qld 4107
Australia
www.boolarongpress.com.au

National Library of Australia Cataloguing-in-Publication entry:

Creator:	Maraun, Gai, author.
Title:	What would you be / Gai Maraun.
ISBN:	9781925522471 (paperback)
Subjects:	Insects–Poetry.

Design by Julie Maraun.

Printed and bound by Watson Ferguson & Company, Salisbury, Brisbane, Australia.

WHAT WOULD YOU BE

If you were an insect what would you be?
A mantis, a cockroach or maybe a flea.
You might say a spider that lives in a loo,
But that's an arachnid so that wouldn't do.

Insects have six legs, arachnids have eight,
So do be careful about whom you date.
Just do a quick leg count before you go out,
With any dark strangers just hanging about.

Insects get eaten and spiders do too,
It's not always easy to know who is who.
So when you're deciding what you'd like to be,
Make sure that you choose most carefully.

Written & Illustrated By
Gai Maraun

BUZZING BEE

Look buzzing bee is making his honey,
Maybe you can have some for your tummy.

He visits the flowers one by one,
As they turn their faces to the sun.

Collecting nectar all day long,
While he sings his happy song.

He steps in the honey sticky and sweet,
And when he gets hungry he licks his feet.

Now bees need nectar to feed their young,
And if you raid their hive you'll likely be stung.

Although a sting hurts and may make you cry,
Remember when they sting it makes them die.

Gai

DANCE OF THE COCKROACH

Oh my, he is so bronze and shiny
Dressed up in all his finery,
So handsome and so sleek
The girls all feel their knees go weak.

While other boys can only mutter
His gossamer wings are all aflutter,
His songs much better than the rest
Will get the girls that he likes best.

His competition admits defeat
As he sweeps those girls right off their feet,
He makes them feel they're best of all
As they all answer to his call.

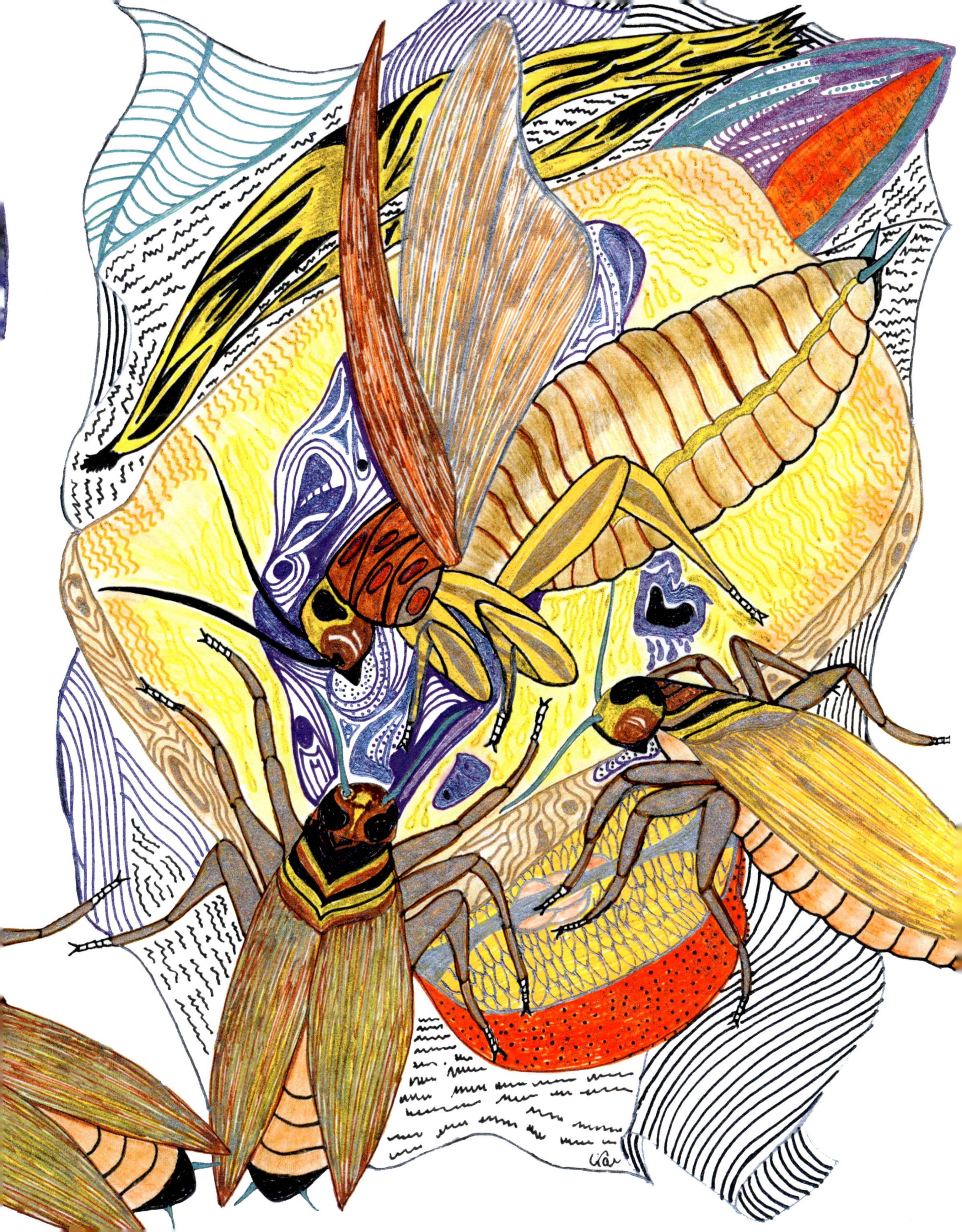

TOWN ANTS

The town ants that live in the garden out back,
Are so industrious there's little they lack.

They care for their nests under house bricks and stones,
And search for snacks among the dog's bones.

In dry times and lean they may come in your house,
Following scent trails which makes mother rouse.

But please don't use poison to send them away,
Just make up sweet water in a bottle to spray.

Around the house and garden beds,
You'll find it turns all the ants' heads.

You might even like to offer a treat,
By putting some sugar out in your street.

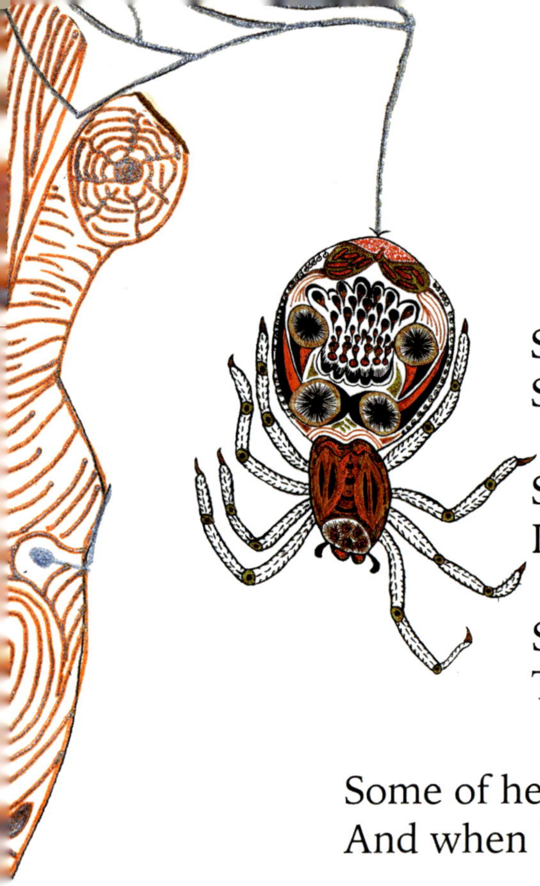

SPIDER WEB

See that spider high in a tree,
She's spinning her web as fine as can be.

She floats on the wind with her invisible thread,
Do you think she could be making her bed?

She spins it at night with incredible care,
To see how many insects she can ensnare.

Some of her threads are covered with glue,
And when bugs make contact there is naught they can do.

She runs down the thread when she feels them vibrate,
And although they may struggle they find it's too late.

She wraps them up in a larder of web,
And sometimes eats them before they are dead.

Gai

LADY BEETLE

Lady beetle all red and black,
Your wings are spotted and you always look fat.

At the break of day you go out to find,
Hundreds of aphids on which you can dine.

You'll find the aphids on fresh veggie leaves,
And when you eat them farmers are pleased.

When the aphids are gone and you've done your best,
You will probably need to enlarge your vest.

THE LOCUST AND THE ANTS

Oh happy Locusts leaping around,
Why is ant watching you with a frown?
He doesn't know how you love to have fun,
Just eating and leaping around in the sun.

Ant is too busy picking up supplies,
For when winters clouds will fill the skies.
He knows so well they will need a full larder,
And that makes them work harder and harder.

But what of the locusts when winters cold,
Spreads over the earth as has been told?
Don't worry their eggs are safely laid,
Down in the ground where they'll be saved.

And when spring comes and the days are warm,
The locusts hatch out and then they swarm.
Leaping and eating without a care,
And sadly they leave the ground quite bare.

So when you see ants busily running around,
You will know that there deep underground.
They have been building up their supplies,
For when those storm clouds fill the skies.

HELICOPTER INSECT

Dragon fly dragon fly hovering high,
What are you doing way up in the sky?

Your wings are so pretty when the sun shines through,
Who would know or have a clue?

That when you are born you look like a grub,
Squishing and squirming in water and mud.

But when it is time to come out of the slime,
You look for a reed that is easy to climb.

You are oh so ugly when first you emerge,
No one would eat you, not even a bird.

But when you dry off and climb out of your shell,
You look so beautiful no one could tell.

That when you were born you looked like that grub,
Just squishing and squirming around in the mud.

THE MANY LEGGED ONE

Who looks for leaves all yellow and brown?
And then waits for them to fall down to the ground.

Who eats dead leaves and old vegetable matter?
That tastes so good but won't make you fatter.

It's me a beautiful shiny millipede,
With many legs but not much speed.

My legs are many and so very neat,
It's hard to see I haven't any feet.

They work so well getting me around,
I just seem to float over the ground.

I don't bite and I don't have a sting,
But I make great nasty stuff under my skin.

So it doesn't matter if I can't run so fast,
Or if in a race I might come last.

And even though I look good to eat,
You may be fooled but I don't taste sweet.

One time I ended up in someone's mouth,
But they very quickly spat me out!

I don't really need any poison or spikes,
For animals to think I am not very nice.

THINK GREEN

She's very long lean and delicate green,
A praying mantis it would seem.

Her little head with big brown eyes,
Will always win favor with the guys.

She swivels her head this way and that,
I wonder just what she is looking at?

She hunts by night and also by day,
Swaying backward and forward awaiting her prey.

Her mate may drop in for a share of her tea,
And sometimes she'll eat him unrepentantly.

Poor thing didn't know that her digestive sauce,
Made him a most delicious main course.

FRUIT FLY

Why has that fruit fly changed her flight?
Is there an apple somewhere in sight?

It is inside the fruit she lays her eggs,
Which hatch into maggots and have no legs.

The apple is all they really need,
To make them grow with incredible speed.

And because they're in deep and out of sight,
You might get a fright if you take a big bite.

WATER WORLD

There is a spider who lives in a bell,
A bell underwater or so I've heard tell.

The bell is spun of silk and is made for her home,
And seen underwater looks a bit like a dome.

When construction is done and she's finished her lair,
She fills up her bell with a bubble of air.

So even an insect that's incredibly brave,
Can end up with bell spider in watery grave.

What Do You Know?

1. BEES = Are bees insects or arachnids and why?

2. COCKROACH = What are the cockroaches eating?

3. HELICOPTER INSECT = How many, fish, tadpoles, dragon fly lava, mosquito wrigglers, mosquitos and jelly fish can you see?

4. SPIDER = How many legs does the spider have and how many insects are caught in her web?

5. LADY BEETLE = How many aphids are left for her to eat?

6. LOCUSTS & THE ANTS = How many ants are there? What is another word for locust?

7. MANY LEGGED ONE = Can you find the reptile, woodlice (crustaceans) and snails(molluscs)?
How many of each?

8. FRUIT FLY = How many legs can you see, how many lava (maggots) can you find?

10. WATER WORLD = How many sea creatures can you see?

11. THINK GREEN = What can happen to the mate of a female praying mantis?

ANSWERS
1. Insects, as they only have six legs.
2. A slice of bread.
3. 6, 6, 2, 5, 4, 2.
4. 8, 3.
5. 4
6. 4, grasshopper.
7. 1, 2 and 4.
8. 4, 17
9. 6
10. He may be eaten.

Gai

Gai
Gai

AUTHOR BIOGRAPHY

Since I was a small child I have had a keen interest in animals, the four, six and eight legged variety. Collecting cicadas, breeding silk worms, the moths of which, threatened my mother's sanity by laying their eggs in every available draw in the house. I also bred white mice which escaped on a regular basis and when they were banned I moved on to budgerigars, which remained caged.
I studied to be a ballet dancer, a nurse for some years, but finally ended up as a sheep farmer.
In between these occupations I spent five years setting up and running the insect breeding department at Taronga Zoo. This included cockroaches, flies and mealworms providing a natural food for small animals, reptiles and birds. This eventually grew to include rats and mice for larger animals.
It was during my child raising years that I first began little drawings and rhymes for the covers of my daughter's school books. Eventually over time I changed the rhymes to include facts, hoping to engage children's interest in these small life forms who share our planet.

With Thanks To My Darling Daughters
For Their Help and Encouragement
and For My Grandson Brandon.

Gai